GO
FUND
YOU

STEPHANIE STERLINGS

ISBN 978-1-7349959-0-9

Printed in the United States of America.

Cover Design by 99designs.com
Interior Design by FormattedBooks.com

Monthly Expenses	Monthly Budget Amount	Monthly Actual Amount	Difference
Housing			
Mortgage or Rent			
Homeowners or Renters Insurance			
Property Taxes			
Association Dues			
Home Repairs			
Landscaping/Housekeeping			
Total			
Utilities			
Electric/Gas/Oil			
Garbage			
Water/Sewer			
Cable/Satellite/Internet			
Phone/Cell Phone			
Netflix/Hulu			
Total			
Debt Repayment			
Vehicle Loan/Lease Payment			
Credit Card			
School Loan			
Other			
Total			
Person			
Toiletries			
Clothing			
Salon/Cosmetics			
Dry Cleanin			
Subscriptions/M			
Pets-Food			
Char			
Gift			

Visit www.gofundyou.online for a free budget template.

DOWNLOAD THE FREE BUDGET TEMPLATE

Just to say thanks for buying my book, I would like to give you the Budget Template 100% FREE

TO DOWNLOAD GO TO:

https://gofundyou.online/budget

CONTENTS

For my son, Anthony

I am so proud of the man you have become. Your commitment to becoming financially literate and achieving financial independence is the reason this book came to be. You've inspired me to teach the same principles to as many others as possible.

I love you.

INTRODUCTION

Long before I had a checking account of my own, my family helped nurture in me a positive relationship with money. My beloved Grandpa Ralph was the first person who sparked my interest in it when I was a young child. Whenever he visited, I'd rush to greet him at the door, squealing with joy as he scooped me up into a warm hug. Then he'd step back, put his hands in his pockets, and regard me with a serious expression—the twinkle in his eye giving him away. His fingers would bounce the loose coins up and down in his pocket, a chorus of soft jingling. It was a sound I came to associate with him, and I was always tantalized by it because I knew what it meant—those coins were for me!

At the end of every visit, he would pull all of his spare change out of his pocket and pour it into my eagerly cupped palms. I took the stairs two at a time as I raced to my bedroom, making straight for my pink ceramic piggy bank. After I had reverently dropped the small collection of pennies, nickels, dimes, and quarters in, one by one, I would shake my little piggy bank, relishing the sound of dozens of coins dancing inside. I gauged the amount of money I'd saved by the weight of my piggy bank; I would shake it several times, my face absorbed in extreme concentration, and I was certain I could *feel* the growth.

Whenever my piggy bank became so full it threatened to burst, my dad and I had a tradition of emptying it onto the polished oak of the kitchen table and counting the coins together. Being a banker, he was the perfect person to assist me. I would record the total and the next day, he would take the coins with him to work for deposit. He would bring the deposit receipt home with him, and it was my responsibility to reconcile the amount on the deposit receipt with the amount I had noted during the counting process.

Grandpa Ralph's spare change—always given freely and with love—as well as my treasured piggy bank were my first experiences with money. To me, everything about money felt natural, fun, and exciting.

Unfortunately, all of those positive associations with money were quickly destroyed after one of Grandpa Ralph's visits.

On that particular day, I told Grandpa Ralph that my piggy bank was almost full and that it felt heavier than ever before! To my surprise, Grandpa Ralph withdrew a crisp five dollar bill from his wallet and handed it to me. We sat together, musing about the various things five dollars could buy, as we folded the bill into a little rectangle, ensuring it would fit into my nearly full piggy bank.

Hardly believing my good luck, I made a beeline for my piggy bank, took it off the shelf, and instantly felt a hollow pit in my stomach. My piggy bank was as light as a feather. I shook it over and over, but it made no sound. "Where did all my money go?" I wondered in despair. I had been so careful in saving every coin, and suddenly, they had all mysteriously disappeared.

Later, my dad told me he had emptied the piggy bank himself and made the deposit on my behalf. He didn't even bring me the deposit receipt. To this day, I don't know what possessed him to break our tradition of counting the money together. He never offered me an explanation, nor did he express any feelings of remorse. All I know is that I felt betrayed and completely disempowered, as if the rug had been ripped right out from under me.

Worse yet, that feeling followed me like a ghost for years.

The incident with my father and the sudden absence of those painstakingly saved coins taught me that I had to stay connected to my money for my own security and peace of mind. When I was a teenager and began earning a wage for the first time as a babysitter and berry picker, I developed a respect toward money that hadn't been there before. In the years since, I've learned countless more lessons about myself, about money, and about the evolving landscape of my relationship with it.

When I had a son, I used all of the knowledge and wisdom in my arsenal to ensure I raised him to have a healthy, positive relationship with money.

For starters, I never laid a hand on his piggy bank. When he got his first part-time job, I encouraged him to set aside $25 from each paycheck for retirement. He was sixteen years old, and though I was a licensed financial advisor by that time, the only reason he followed my advice was because I was his mom! When he received a raise soon afterward, I suggested he increase his savings to $50 per paycheck. He protested loudly. It was hard advice to follow, but he did it, and this is how he benefited from those savings habits he formed early on:

- He paid cash for a "cool" car while he was still in high school
- He bought a home and obtained a mortgage when he was 20 years old
- He had $100,000 saved for retirement by the time he was 27 years old

These achievements may seem out of reach, but anyone, regardless of age, can start now and achieve similar goals. It requires discipline and a willingness to take full responsibility for your financial plan, but it could mean the difference between scant retirement years and extraordinary wealth.

I am completely convinced that the chapters ahead will help you understand where and how to begin so that during your retirement years, you can be the one with plenty of jingling coins that captivate the young minds in your life.

CHAPTER ONE
BUDGETING

PAYING FOR PRIORITIES

When my son was in high school, he learned how to budget. In the beginning, he didn't have a firm grasp on how he was spending his money each month. He was basically just playing a guessing game. I came up with a simple way to help him track his purchases. I provided him with a large envelope and asked him to collect all of his receipts in there for an entire month.

At the end of the month, he sorted those receipts into categories such as gasoline, dining out, entertainment, and so forth. Together, we reviewed his findings, and I asked him what he had learned from the exercise. He realized he ate out too much and needed to make his own food more often to cut down on spending.

How much did you earn last month? How much did you spend?

Those are pretty straightforward questions, but whenever I invoke the word "budget" to ask the same things, I notice that people's eyes tend to spin, they become overwhelmed, or they sheepishly admit they have no idea.

Budgeting is essentially the act of balancing how much money you earn and how much money you spend each month. Spending more than you earn is a dangerous pattern that will surely put you into debt. Hopefully you brought in at least as much money as went out—ideally more. Still, there are times when there's just too much *month* and not enough *money* to last!

Actively budgeting allows you to remain aware of your spending, work your way out of existing debt, avoid taking on more debt, save for the things you really want, and ultimately become rich! Without budgeting, you won't truly know where your money is going or what you are spending it on, even if you think you do. I guarantee you'll feel more in control by knowing what your expenses are and paying close attention to your spending habits.

Take a moment to think about what you really want. Are you willing to do what it takes to achieve that goal? How badly do you want to achieve it?

DISCOVERING YOUR PATTERNS

Everyone's personal budget is unique. Most people know how much their recurring monthly expenses are, including rent or a mortgage payment, their phone bill, and their gym membership. However, most people don't realize how much they spend on dining out, movies, Starbucks, alcohol, groceries, gas, etc. Once you add up how much money you are spending on restaurants and entertainment per year, you might be shocked.

This is where you need to get down to the nitty gritty details and dial in your budget. If you are serious about wanting to achieve your financial goals and save for the things you dream about, you must first figure out where every penny goes. The first step is to gather all of your most recent bank statements and credit card statements.

Once you've done that, decide upon specific spending categories. The list of categories will vary from person to person but typically includes things like groceries, gas, entertainment, personal goods, clothing, utilities, dining out, travel, pets, and so on. Try to avoid a "miscellaneous" category.

Then track each expense listed on your bank and credit card statements under the corresponding category. This will take some time, and you may need to tweak your categories, but once you're done, total each category.

This activity can be a real eye-opener; you'll find out quickly what your spending personality is. Some people discover they eat out way too much and it would be more cost-effective to prepare their own meals. Maybe you're one of those people who buys coffee on a daily basis, too many rounds at the bar, or a slew of games on your smartphone. Others may determine that the car they are driving is costing them a small fortune in repairs or gas, and that it might be time to consider a more economical or reliable vehicle. Perhaps you spend too much on clothes and shoes, or you have an expensive hobby. Whatever the case may be, it is time to face the facts.

ACCOUNTABILITY

Determine where your weaknesses are when it comes to spending. Take ownership of your spending habits and don't blame others or make excuses for your financial circumstances. The good news is you can make the necessary adjustments to change the direction of your spending immediately. You might decide that a caramel macchiato is not necessary every day and instead treat yourself to one every week or two. By thoughtfully reducing your spending in nonessential categories, you will free up money for other things like building up emergency savings, paying off debt, and saving for your goals.

Budgeting is the single most important factor to ensuring financial success! Get going now and take the time to:

1. Gather your most recent bank and credit card statements
2. Create categories for your budget

3. Track each expense from your statements under the corresponding category
4. Calculate the total of each category
5. Be honest with yourself about your spending habits and challenge yourself to make adjustments accordingly
6. Moving forward, continue tracking your expenses this way to keep yourself accountable

You can create a budget with pen and paper, you can utilize an elaborate spreadsheet, or you can choose any number of options in between—as long as it works for you. There's a plethora of resources including books, blogs, YouTube videos, podcasts, websites like Mint.com, and smartphone apps to further assist you with budgeting. You can even use software such as Quicken Personal Finance or You Need a Budget (YNAB).

Here is a sample budget template for you...

Monthly Expenses	Monthly Budget Amount	Monthly Actual Amount	Difference
Housing			
Mortgage or Rent			
Homeowners or Renters Insurance			
Property Taxes			
Association Dues			
Home Repairs			
Landscaping/Housekeeping			
Total			
Utilities			
Electric/Gas/Oil			
Garbage			
Water/Sewer			
Cable/Satellite/Internet			
Phone/Cell Phone			
Netflix/Hulu			
Total			
Debt Repayment			
Vehicle Loan/Lease Payment			
Credit Card			
School Loan			
Other			
Total			
Persor			
Toiletries			
Clothing			
Salon/Cosmetics			
Dry Cleanin			
Subscriptions/M			
Pets-Foor			
Char			
Gift			

Visit www.gofundyou.online for a free budget template.

Visit www.gofundyou.online for a FREE budget template.

CHAPTER TWO
GOALS

DESIGNING AND LIVING YOUR COMPELLING FUTURE

When he was much younger, I felt it was important to help my son feel excited about goal-setting. Whenever he received money, either his allowance or on a special occasion, he would spend it right away on things like Pokémon cards and Lego sets.

One year, right before his birthday, I took him to a large department store. As we walked around the store together, I asked him to carefully consider what one thing he would buy there if he could get anything he wanted.

After wandering around and looking at everything with a new perspective (since nothing was out of reach in this hypothetical scenario), he picked out a sleek silver and neon yellow bicycle. I explained encouragingly that if he set a goal to buy the bicycle, he could achieve that goal by avoiding smaller purchases like the trading cards and toy sets. "If you save that money instead of spending it," I told him, "you can afford something bigger and more meaningful."

He did just that. Three months later, we returned to the store so he could buy the bicycle he had picked out, proudly handing a pile of crumpled bills to the smiling cashier.

Now that you have a firm grasp on your budget, it is time to consider your goals. Goals are essentially dreams with deadlines.

THE IMPORTANCE OF GOALS

Let's face it: you can't just think to yourself, "*I want a private jet!*" and expect it to magically appear. The same is true when planning for retirement. It doesn't just happen, even if you already have a frugal mindset.

Consider what your life could look like five years from now and don't be afraid to dream a little! Looking ahead, ponder these questions:

* Where do I stand financially?
* What debt do I have?
* How much money is in my emergency fund?
* Am I a homeowner?
* Am I making donations to a charity that's close to my heart?
* Am I putting money into my child's college fund?
* What, specifically, allows me to feel financially secure and successful?

These are just a few questions to get you thinking about what you want to achieve within a certain timeframe. Now come back to the present moment and look at your current financial situation. What steps can you take now to achieve that ideal life in five years' time?

THE COMPONENTS OF A GOAL

Over the years, I've learned many goal-setting techniques. The one I find most useful is the S.M.A.R.T. method, created by George T. Doran in 1981. He used the acronym S.M.A.R.T. to illustrate the five main components of setting a goal:

- **S**pecific: target a specific area for improvement
- **M**easurable: quantify, or at least suggest, an indicator of progress
- **A**ssignable: delegate to a specific person or team
- **R**ealistic: identify what results can realistically be achieved, given available resources
- **T**ime-related: state specifically when the result can be achieved

I'm grateful to Mr. Doran for his S.M.A.R.T. model. Through life experience and real-world application, I have taken his method and made it my own. I call it: S.M.A.R.T.E.R.

- **S**pecific: When setting a goal, it is important that it be very clear and well-defined. It cannot be vague!
- **M**easurable: Choose a specific dollar amount, or other unit of measure as needed.
- **A**ttainable: Is this something you honestly believe you can achieve? Your goal should not be impossible but not too easy either; it should challenge you.
- **R**elevant: Make sure your goal aligns with your values, priorities, career, and the desired direction of your life.
- **T**ime-related: Your goal must have a deadline. Choosing a date of completion in advance encourages you to stay focused.
- **E**valuate: Check in with yourself often on your journey. Be completely honest with yourself. If you are stuck, figure out what is holding you back.
- **R**evise: Instead of giving up or surrendering, just make adjustments to your behavior or approach and forge ahead. Obstacles and roadblocks will always come up—that's life! Adapting and finding ways to maneuver around them is a hallmark of any successful goal-setter.

Here is an example of a S.M.A.R.T.E.R. goal created in December:

Specific: I will deposit $6,000 into my individual retirement account next year.

Measurable: I will have $250 from each of my semi-monthly paychecks direct-deposited into the individual retirement account.

Attainable: Based on my current income, and by budgeting and spending wisely, I can reasonably set aside $500 each month.

Relevant: It's important to me that my retirement years are comfortable so that I can travel the world and spoil my grandkids.

Time-related: I will achieve this goal in twelve months (by December 31st).

Evaluate: I will check my retirement account statement at the end of each month to ensure the $500 was deposited.

Revise: I will periodically assess my progress and make adjustments as needed.

HOW TO SET A GOAL

You must write down your goal. Putting pen to paper isn't necessary; saving it on your computer or in your smartphone is perfectly fine. Give careful consideration to the specific language you use in formulating your goals. Use positive, active verbs like "I will" rather than more passive phrases such as "I would like to." A clear, definitive goal is much more motivating because it's phrased as if you have absolutely no choice but to accomplish it.

I suggest posting handwritten or printed copies of your goal on your wall, bathroom mirror, desk, computer monitor, or refrigerator. You might even want to find a picture that represents your goal and make it the lock screen on your smartphone or a screensaver on your computer—for instance, a photo of a sandy beach if you're saving for a trip to Bali.

Once you have defined your goal, create an action plan by listing each small step that needs to be accomplished. An action plan for the example shared earlier might look like this:

- Research five financial institutions where I can open an individual retirement account and narrow down the list until I find one that is a good fit.
- Open an individual retirement account at the selected financial institution.
- Contact my company's HR department to set up direct deposit to the new retirement account in the amount of $250 per paycheck.
- Review my budget and adjust my spending priorities, as I will effectively have $250 less to spend each pay period.

Place goal deadlines, milestones, and reminders in or on your calendar. There should be a recurring date at least monthly when you evaluate (and, if needed, revise) your goal. Checking your progress often is crucial to your success. You can automate certain aspects of your action plan (e.g., setting up direct deposit) for the sake of convenience, but the mentality of "set it and forget it" does not apply to goal-setting!

Give it some thought. Where would you like to be in five, ten, or twenty years? What S.M.A.R.T.E.R. goals are you going to set for yourself to get there? Start now!

ONE YEAR GOALS

1. CREATE AND STICK WITH A BUDGET
2. MEAL PLAN EACH WEEK
3. OPEN A RETIREMENT ACCOUNT
4. LOOK INTO WORK RETIREMENT PLAN
5. BUILD AN EMERGENCY FUND
6. GET A WILL
7. START A SAVINGS ACCOUNT FOR DOWN PAYMENT ON A HOUSE
8. CREATE PLAN TO PAYOFF CREDIT CARDS

FIVE YEAR GOALS

1. BUY A HOUSE
2. TAKE A TRIP TO BALI
3. ADOPT A RESCUE DOG

CHAPTER THREE
CREDIT

GETTING CREDIT WHEN CREDIT IS DUE

Credit tends to be a murky topic, and there's a heavy stigma and a lot of misinformation surrounding it. I know one young man who closed his oldest credit card because he thought it was just the same as closing a checking or savings account. He didn't realize it would impact the length of his credit history and therefore cause his score to drop. Similarly, a young woman I met was distraught to learn two store credit cards she had were eventually closed by the issuing credit card companies simply because she hadn't used them in a while. She didn't know that in order to prevent her credit card accounts from being systematically closed, she needed to use those credit cards every so often. Her credit score dropped as a result of her credit history length effectively shortening, and when she applied for a home loan not too long afterward, the interest rate was higher than she had been expecting.

WHAT IS CREDIT?

When an entity chooses to extend credit to you, that means it is lending you money because it trusts you to eventually repay that borrowed money (with interest). You must earn that trust over time; it is not readily given. While relatives and friends may trust you because they know you, a financial institution makes a determination about your creditworthiness before letting you borrow money. It views your credit history in order to make that determination. We'll come back to that later.

Credit can be "unsecured" or "secured." Unsecured credit is when you either don't have collateral or haven't offered it to the lender in the event that you can't repay the borrowed money. Secured credit is collateralized, which means that if you can't repay the borrowed money, the lender is able to fall back on the value of your property (often a house or car) to make itself whole.

Most everyone will utilize some form of unsecured or secured credit in their lifetime, typically in the form of auto loans, student loans, credit cards, mortgages, or lines of credit. You may not have a credit history yet, so I will explain the steps for initially obtaining credit, and then subsequently building it.

HOW DO I OBTAIN CREDIT FOR THE FIRST TIME?

A great way to begin establishing credit is by applying for a secured credit card as early as your 18th birthday. With a secured credit card, you offer the bank collateral (in this case, cash) by making an upfront deposit. The amount you give the bank will be the credit limit on the secured credit card they issue you. For example, if you deposited $500 upfront, you would then be able to charge up to $500 on the card (a $500 spending limit).

Most credit cards are unsecured, but in order to obtain an unsecured credit card, you need to have a good credit history. When you have no credit history, the bank views you as a risk, so you eliminate that risk by providing a deposit upfront. Once you've had the secured credit card for a while and have consistently made payments on time, you can ask the bank if it will convert your secured credit card to an unsecured credit card.

TYPES OF CREDIT

There are two types of credit: installment and revolving.

"Installment" refers to loans of a fixed amount, often with a fixed interest rate, resulting in predictable periodic payment amounts. Home and auto loans fall under this category. With an installment loan, you agree to make a set number of payments at a specific dollar amount each month. The repayment period on an installment loan will last until the loan is fully paid off (with interest), whether it takes months or years.

"Revolving" refers to credit that does not have a fixed dollar amount or number of payments. Credit cards fall under this category. Let's say you have a credit card with a $1,000 limit, and you purchased concert tickets worth $300. Since the tickets were bought on credit rather than with cash, it's considered "borrowing" until that $300 is repaid.

You can choose to either pay off the entire $300 balance at the end of the month (resulting in no interest charges) or pay the minimum amount dictated by the credit card company (let's say it's $25) and carry the unpaid portion of your balance ($275) from month to month until you pay it off. Keep in mind you will almost always incur an (oftentimes hefty) interest charge for carrying a balance on your credit card.

CREDIT REPORT VS. CREDIT SCORE

Most lenders and creditors obtain your credit history from credit reporting agencies. The three major credit bureaus in the United States are Equifax, Experian, and TransUnion. These are for-profit companies that are not affiliated with the government. However, the government passed legislation called the Fair Credit Reporting Act that protects consumers from having inaccurate information permanently documented on their credit reports.

One of the most well-known credit scorers is Fair Isaac Corporation (FICO). The FICO score is the score most creditors use when evaluating creditworthiness. All of the information in your credit report is boiled down to a three-digit number between 300 and 850. Your creditworthiness (rank) is determined by the range in which your credit score falls:

Rank	Range
Exceptional	800–850
Very Good	740–799
Good	670–739
Fair	580–669
Poor	300–579

The formula used to convert your credit history into a single score is proprietary information, so we have no way of knowing exactly what it is. Still, we *do* know there are five main factors that determine a person's FICO score. Let's explore each one and see what percentage of a score each factor comprises.

WHAT FACTORS MAKE UP A CREDIT SCORE?

1. **35% Payment History**
   This is the record of whether you've made payments on time or late (and *how* late). The more recent, severe, and frequent a late payment is, the greater the negative impact on your score. The single most important step you can take with regard to credit is to make every single payment on time.

2. **30% Credit Usage**
   Creditors will look at how much of your available credit you're using, how many of your accounts have balances, and what the balance of your installment loan is now compared to the amount initially loaned. Ideally, keep the ending balance on your monthly credit card statement between 1% and 10% of that card's credit limit. For instance, try not to let your ending balance exceed $100 on a credit card with

15

a $1,000 credit limit. Balances over 10% of the limit will start to decrease your credit score. Balances over 30% of the credit limit will cause your score to drop fairly aggressively. Balances over 90% of the credit limit will have only a negative effect on your credit score. Using the majority of your available credit is a red flag to future lenders. It seems counterintuitive, but lenders like seeing that you *don't* use most of the credit you're extended. This is because they are wary of your ability to make future payments if it appears you rely heavily on credit to pay for things.

3. **15% Length of Credit History**
   Creditors will take into consideration how long you have had your credit accounts open—both revolving and installment. The longer your credit history, the better, so think long and hard before closing your oldest credit card! Doing so will decrease the average age of all your open credit accounts and will cause your score to drop.

4. **10% New Credit**
   This factor relates to how many new credit accounts you've recently opened, or tried to open. Lenders don't like seeing that you've opened or attempted to open a bunch of accounts in the recent past because it points to an urgent need for more credit.

5. **10% Credit Mix**
   Lenders like to see a healthy mix of both installment and revolving accounts. For instance, a person with a mortgage, a student loan, an auto loan, and two credit cards will be viewed more favorably than a person with five credit cards.

WHY DOES CREDIT MATTER?

Credit is a vital part of your overall financial health. Your credit history and score will determine whether or not you're approved for a credit account. If your credit score is very good or exceptional, you'll be approved for a lower interest rate than someone with a fair or good score, ultimately reducing the amount you have to pay each month on an installment loan.

It is really important to manage credit well. It takes a long time of responsible credit usage to increase your credit score, but it takes as little as one late payment to make your score drop dramatically overnight.

HOW CAN I IMPROVE MY SCORE?

Don't be discouraged if your score isn't quite what you would like it to be. You can't change the past, but you can start now and make positive changes moving forward. Reestablishing healthy credit habits will pay off as your credit score reflects recent payment patterns. Here are some things you can do to help improve your score:

1. Check your credit report for inaccurate information and work to have any errors corrected or eradicated. This can be done on your own, or you can hire a company to do it on your behalf. If you work with a company, do your research to ensure it's reputable and you aren't being scammed.
2. Keep your oldest credit account open, even if you are not actively using it. Do not close it unless you really must! Make one purchase on the card every so often (every six to twelve months) to prevent the card issuer from closing the account due to lack of use.
3. Reduce the amount of your credit balances when possible. Don't get carried away trying to collect credit card reward points; nearly maxing out a card for the reward points isn't worth it, as you'll be paying far more in interest charges than you're earning in points!
4. Ensure your bills are paid on time by setting up payment reminders and/or automatic bill pay from your bank account.
5. Don't allow any person or entity to make a hard credit inquiry unless it is truly necessary. There are two types

of inquiries: hard and soft. A hard inquiry is when you authorize a creditor to "pull" your credit, and this type of inquiry *will* appear on your credit report regardless of whether or not you're approved. Hard inquiries impact the "New Credit" factor described earlier, though the older an inquiry, the less impact it has on your score, and they eventually fall off your credit report altogether. A soft inquiry is when you pull your own credit report, or when an entity pulls your credit report without your authorization. (If you've ever seen or received offers in the mail saying you're "preapproved" for a certain credit card, it's likely that the company extending the offer has performed a soft inquiry.) A soft inquiry does not show up on your credit report, nor will it affect your score.

Once every 12 months, you're legally entitled to a free credit report from each of the three credit reporting agencies (Equifax, Experian, and TransUnion). You can order them all at once, or you might opt for viewing one every four months to give you an ongoing picture of your credit.

Access your free credit reports by visiting AnnualCreditReport. com. Keep in mind these free credit reports don't include your credit *score*. Luckily, there are now more ways to access the score itself than ever before. Many banks and credit unions now offer your free FICO score on a monthly basis and some credit card companies will even include your score on your monthly statement. There are free credit-tracking websites and apps that provide an updated score as often as weekly, however, check to see if they use the FICO score or a less common type of score.

CHAPTER FOUR

MANAGING DEBT

GETTING YOUR WHIRLWIND OF BILLS UNDER CONTROL

I had a friend who, in his twenties, would constantly tell me he was broke. He didn't use it as an excuse, nor did he seem to be ashamed to say it, but it did prevent him from doing things like celebrating his buddy's birthday at a seafood buffet, fixing the muffler on his motorcycle, and buying tickets to the local summer music festival. He was a hard worker and had a good job, so I had difficulty understanding why he kept saying he was broke. The next time he declared, "I'm broke!" I gently questioned him about it. He shared with me that he had some debt and various never-ending bills, and that he felt like he was always in the hole every single month, living paycheck to paycheck.

I offered to help him come up with a plan so he could get a handle on his debt and achieve some financial goals. We went over his finances together and came up with a budget. He finally had a clearer picture of how much money he was making and how much debt he owed. With this information, I put together a detailed pay-off schedule utilizing the snowball technique that I will cover in this chapter. Less than a year later, he was working to eliminate the very last of his debt. I was so proud of him when he achieved his goal of buying his first home before he turned thirty.

WHAT IS DEBT?

Debt is money owed by one party to another. Debt can also be referred to as a liability. The party who loans money (the lender) generally agrees to do so under the condition that the full amount is to be paid back by the borrower at a later date, usually with interest.

GETTING A HANDLE ON DEBT

I believe most everyone wants to be debt-free, however, getting a handle on your debt can be overwhelming and tricky. The first step is to make a complete list of all your debts. Include credit card balances, student loans, auto loans, mortgages, installment payments on a cell phone purchase, the $750 you borrowed from your cousin, etc. List the name of each lender, the balance owed, the interest rate you are paying, and the typical minimum monthly payment.

Next, you need to decide what debt to pay off first. If you have collections or charge-offs from old debts, you will need to pay those off first. While you are paying these off, you still need to keep making minimum payments toward all other debt.

If you're struggling to make payments, you need to take action quickly. Call your creditors to find out if there are additional options available to you. Your options will vary depending upon the type of loans you have.

If you are offered a loan modification, get the details in writing before proceeding. If the debt is old, there's a good chance that the creditor will accept a lesser amount than the balance. You might qualify for deferment or forbearance if you have student loans. Both options pause payments on your loan. If you qualify for deferment, the government covers the interest costs of the subsidized loans. If you're granted forbearance, the interest keeps accruing and you'll have to pay it eventually. Credit card companies and mortgage and auto lenders may be willing to work out a payment plan if the payments become unaffordable for you.

It's up to you to be proactive, stay on top of your debt, and try to negotiate your debt amounts and terms whenever possible.

METHODS FOR PAYING DOWN YOUR DEBT MORE QUICKLY

Are you paying extra toward all of your debt, over and above the minimum payment? That's commendable and certainly speaks volumes to your commitment to become debt-free sooner rather than later, but paying a little bit extra on every debt usually isn't very effective. Instead, two of the methods I highly recommend are the Debt Snowball and the Debt Avalanche.

Here are the four steps of the Debt Snowball method:

1. Sort your list of debts by "balance owed" from smallest to largest.
2. Make minimum payments on all of your debts *except* the one with the smallest balance.
3. Pay as much as possible in addition to the minimum payment on your smallest debt.
4. Once you eliminate the smallest debt, move on to the next smallest. Keep repeating steps 1–3 until all of your debts are paid in full.

The Debt Avalanche method works a little differently. With this version, sort your list of debts by "interest rate" from highest to lowest. Instead of paying extra on the smallest balance, you'll pay extra on the debt with the highest interest rate first, and once that's eliminated, you'll pay extra on the debt with the next highest interest rate, and so on.

With both of these methods, you are making minimum payments on all of the debts except the one you're focusing on. The more you can devote toward extra payments, the sooner you'll be out of debt.

The Debt Avalanche method is a popular method for repaying debt because you save money in the long run by targeting the debt with the highest interest rate. The potential tradeoff (depending on your priorities) is that you might not experience the excitement that accompanies the building momentum of the Debt Snowball. Choose whichever method you prefer. The unfortunate truth is that paying off debt can be a painfully slow process. Your progress really depends upon your level of motivation and your willingness to endure short-term sacrifices for long-term goals.

DEBT RELIEF

Debt relief can involve changing your interest rate or payment schedule, lowering your minimum payments, persuading creditors to agree to accept less than the full amount owed, or wiping out debt altogether through bankruptcy.

There are several ways you can obtain debt relief:

- Bankruptcy
- Debt settlement
- Debt management
- Do-it-yourself methods, including debt consolidation

Bankruptcy and debt settlement can reduce or eliminate your debts altogether, but they can severely impact your credit. If you go this route, be aware that there are some types of debt that typically can't be erased or reduced (such as federal student loans, child support, and secured loans on vehicles and homes).

A debt management plan allows you to pay your unsecured debts, like credit cards, in full, but often at a reduced interest rate or with fees waived. Typically, you make a single payment each month to a credit counseling agency. The credit counseling agency will then distribute your payment among the creditors that you owe. Credit counselors have debt management agreements in place with credit card companies that benefit their clients.

Credit counseling provides guidance and support on consumer credit, money and debt management, and budgeting. The objective of most credit counseling companies is to help you avoid bankruptcy and to provide you with financial education (specifically with regard to managing money).

There are many not-for-profit credit counseling organizations that offer services at local offices, online, and over the phone. Many universities, military bases, credit unions, housing authorities, and branches of the US Cooperative Extension Service operate nonprofit credit counseling programs. Local financial institutions and consumer protection agencies may also be a good source of information and referrals. "Not-for-profit" doesn't necessarily mean that the services are free, affordable, or legitimate. Some credit counseling organizations charge high (and possibly hidden) fees.

The National Foundation for Credit Counseling (NFCC) and the Association of Independent Consumer Credit Counseling Agencies (AICCCA) list legitimate credit counseling services across the United States.

If you decide to get relief through a debt management plan, your credit card accounts will be closed and, in most cases, you'll have to live without credit cards until you can complete the plan. The debt management plan itself does not affect your credit score, but closing accounts can hurt your score. In addition, missing payments can knock you out of the plan.

There are debt relief companies out there that promise to help if you're struggling. Be careful; many of these are scams. They charge a fee but often do very little work, which ultimately doesn't end up helping you eliminate your debt. If you want to use a debt relief company, view its ratings and reviews on the Better Business Bureau website.

If you decide to do it yourself, you can do what the credit counselors do. You can create your own debt management plan by contacting your creditors, explaining your situation, and negotiating a plan to catch up. Most credit card companies have hardship programs, and they may be willing to lower your interest rates.

There may also be more traditional debt payoff strategies that are available to you. For example, if your credit score is still good, you may qualify for a credit card with a zero interest balance transfer offer that can give you some breathing room. Just remember that the zero interest is usually available only for a limited amount of time.

Debt consolidation loans allow borrowers to roll multiple debts into a single new debt with a fixed monthly payment and, ideally, a lower interest rate. Keep in mind this does not get rid of your debt; it just moves it from one creditor to another. In other words, you're just moving your debt from one bucket to another bucket. The bottom line is that you still are holding a bucket of debt.

Typically, these options won't hurt your credit. As long as you make the payments on time, your credit score should rebound.

Regardless of how you choose to handle your debt, it is incredibly important to have a plan in place that will prevent you from running up a significant amount of debt again right after you get done working so diligently to pay it all off! Don't underestimate how much your behavior and your financial mindset contribute to that plan.

GRATITUDE AND OTHER DEBTS

I'd like you to take a moment to broaden your thoughts about the nature of debt. Sure, debt is money owed by one party to another; however, I want you to think about debt on a more meaningful level. For example, maybe you owe your parents appreciation for all the love and support they've given you over the years. Maybe you owe your mentor thanks for the coaching that has gotten you where you are today. Maybe you owe your grandparents appreciation for the wisdom they've bestowed on you over the years. Maybe you owe a debt of gratitude to the college you attended for equipping you with the knowledge to pursue your dream job.

Repaying a debt isn't always a bad thing, and it isn't always about money.

CHAPTER FIVE

DEEP IN DEBT

HOW TO CONSTRUCT A LIFE VEST TO ESCAPE A TIDAL WAVE OF DEBT

A young woman I know, Cynthia, was paying extra money toward all of her student loans each month. She was stressed and felt like she wasn't gaining any ground. We worked together to build a plan to use the Debt Snowball on her student loans. Meanwhile, she was able to set aside some savings for an emergency. She was also able to put money into an account every month that was earmarked for retirement. Over the course of a few years, I watched her eliminate several of her student loans and even purchase her first home. This was all a result of careful planning and commitment.

Managing your debt and saving for your future at the same time is possible! You just need dedication and drive. Make a plan and stick to it.

DEBT-TO-INCOME RATIO

Your debt-to-income ratio comes into play when you're applying for a mortgage. This ratio compares the amount you owe to the amount you earn. There are a couple of ways it can be calculated. One way is to add up your debt balances and compare that to your annual income. The other way is to add up your monthly debt payments and compare that to your monthly income.

Knowing your debt-to-income ratio will help you determine if your debt could disqualify you from borrowing money in the future. For example, if you want to apply for a mortgage, you usually won't qualify if your debt-to-income ratio is higher than 43%. Lenders prefer to see that ratio below 36%, with no more than 28% of that debt going toward your mortgage payment. For example, assume your gross income is $4,000 per month. A monthly mortgage payment that is 28% of your debt would be $1,120 ($4,000 × 0.28 = $1,120). Your lender will also look at the total of your monthly debt payments, which should not exceed 36%, or in this case, $1,440 per month ($4,000 × 0.36 = $1,440).

If you have a high debt-to-income ratio, you'll have a harder time finding a company that is willing to lend you money. Calculate your debt-to-income ratio and, if necessary, take steps to reduce your debt load. Not only will it show lenders that you have responsibly reduced or eliminated debt obligations, but it will certainly improve your overall financial health.

NEEDS VS. WANTS

As I mentioned before, reducing debt can take time, and that is why it is so important to consider *needs* versus *wants* when you are deciding how to spend money. Needs are things you must have in order to survive like food, shelter, healthcare, and transportation. Wants are things you would like to have but you don't need to survive like Starbucks coffee, movies, dining out, new clothes, smartphone game apps, etc.

If you're a compulsive shopper and you truly struggle with keeping your spending habits under control, you can get help through Debtors Anonymous. Debtors Anonymous is a free support group for people who need help controlling their compulsive debt accumulation. There are no fees or membership dues required to join, but members can make donations to help support the group. The only requirement for joining is that you commit to stop taking on unsecured debt. Attending the meetings will give you the chance to speak to other people in the same situation and learn new habits needed to effect a major lifestyle change. Still, going to a meeting isn't enough. You must take ownership of your compulsive spending and use the tools at your disposal to turn your spending around.

DEALING WITH DEBT COLLECTORS

Dealing with creditors and credit reporting agencies is sometimes overwhelming and confusing, but being bombarded by debt collectors can be very scary and intimidating. They are relentless.

Many people don't know that there are certain laws that govern debt collectors. If they overstep the law, you can file a complaint about them with the Federal Trade Commission (FTC). You can also ask a debt collector to stop calling you. Legally, they must stop. If they do not, you can report them to the FTC. Here are the laws that collectors must follow:

- They may only call between the hours of 8:00 a.m. to 9:00 p.m. (local time).
- They cannot talk to anyone else about your debt.
- They can only talk to someone else to find out your address, home phone number, or place of employment.
- They cannot harass you (e.g., cuss at you, threaten to hurt you).
- They cannot lie to you.
- They must send you a written notice about your debt called a "quote validation notice." This notice must clearly state the exact amount of money that you owe and who you owe the money to. It should also tell you what to do if you think you do not owe the money.

Dealing with debt collectors isn't anyone's idea of a good time, but you can usually settle an old debt for pennies on the dollar. If you're able to negotiate a lump sum payment to clear this debt, get an agreement in writing first. Never give them electronic access to your bank accounts so they can withdraw the money!

CHAPTER SIX
YOU NEED A WILL

PREPARING FOR THE BIG "WHAT IF"

Remember that friend of mine who always claimed he was broke? He took my advice, began living on a budget, snowballed his debt, and eventually bought his first house. Shortly after that, he was killed in a tragic accident. He was not married and did not have a last will and testament. Because he did not have a will in place, his estate went into probate. While his parents were deep in the trenches of grief, they were burdened with handling his estate, which needed to occur before they could access his belongings—including his house.

WHAT IS A WILL?

A will is a legal document that states your final wishes regarding the distribution of your property and the care of any minor children you may have. According to USA.gov, you must be eighteen or older to write a legally valid will in most states.

I'M YOUNG...DO I REALLY NEED ONE?

In our teens, twenties, and even thirties, we tend to feel invincible and, frankly, not very cognizant of our own mortality. Having a will drawn up isn't something you typically think about at that age. It may even feel a bit morbid thinking about death or worrying about becoming terminally ill or being killed in an accident. Unfortunately, accidents, injuries, and illnesses can happen to someone at any age. That is why it is important to make your wishes known, whether you're an octogenarian or just graduating from high school.

The age at which you decide to write a will is a personal decision, however, there are certain practical considerations that can help you determine when the time is right. For example, if your family has a history of illness or dementia, it might be wise to be proactive when you are younger so you can plan ahead. You must be mentally competent when writing your will.

When you are young, it might seem at first glance that you don't have much in the way of assets, but you probably have some savings, personal belongings, or a car. Digital assets may be especially important. Your will could include access to photos, blogs, music, movies, podcasts, video games, PayPal or Venmo accounts, and other digital aspects of your life.

If you are an unmarried person without children and you were to die without having a will in place, your assets would typically go to your parents. Think about this for a moment. Maybe you were raised by one parent and you do not have a relationship with the other parent. You may not want your belongings or assets to go to both of your parents. There may be groups, charities, or other people to whom you would like to leave assets. Creating a will can serve to definitively make your wishes known.

WHERE DO I START?

Here's how to get started creating your own will:

1. Decide if you want to use an estate attorney or a do-it-yourself website.
2. Select your beneficiaries (the term for people or charities you want to inherit your money or belongings).
3. Ensure the beneficiaries you name in your will match the beneficiaries on your investment and/or retirement accounts. Having a will doesn't mean you don't need to have beneficiaries on your accounts.
4. Choose an executor for your will. The executor is the person that will make sure the wishes in your will are carried out.
5. Choose a guardian to care for your kids and have a discussion with them to confirm they are willing to act in that capacity if needed. A guardian becomes a substitute parental figure for your children should you die, become incapacitated, or otherwise become unable to take care of them.
6. Be specific about who inherits which things. This can be especially tricky when you have more than one child and if you have stepchildren. Be realistic about who gets what; not everything can be distributed equally.
7. You may want to attach a letter to the will. Sometimes a personal letter is a good way to say goodbye and make your wishes clearer and more personal.
8. Typically, two witnesses will need to sign the will. Your witnesses will need to be at least 18 years old. Usually, the witnesses cannot be people who stand to inherit anything in the will.
9. Find a suitable location for your will. It is best to keep your will in a place where it will not be forgotten and can be easily accessed. For example, I keep my original will in a fire safe. I also provided a copy to my son along with a personal

note that includes my wishes. Think twice before placing your will in a safety deposit box only you can access!

10. Review and update your will after any major life event, such as a marriage, divorce, or birth of a child. Otherwise, you may risk leaving all of your assets to, say, your ex-spouse and nothing to your children!

Once you've accomplished these ten steps, you'll already be more prepared than the average person when it comes to legacy and estate planning. Still, there are a few more things that are very helpful to have prepared. A will describes how your assets and property will be distributed when you die, but it does not include where the assets are located or how to get to them. It's best not to cause unnecessary stress for your loved ones when you are gone. Instead, provide these additional pieces of information as an informal addendum to your will:

1. List of all your financial accounts (with full account numbers) including credit cards, bank accounts, investment accounts, student loans, auto loans, and mortgages.
2. List of login credentials for your online accounts, including email. It's best to keep this list secured but accessible.
3. List of your investments including stocks, bonds, mutual funds, ETFs, annuities, retirement accounts, life insurance policies, and the contact information of your insurance agent and/or financial advisor.
4. Leave instructions for your funeral or memorial service. You don't want to completely leave the decision-making in the hands of your family members or friends. I know the importance of this firsthand. When my mom passed away, she had not expressed her final wishes and I, as executor, had to make decisions without knowing if they were what she wanted. Tell your family what you want to happen when you die. You can also allocate funds to pay for your funeral expenses.

Discuss everything with the relevant parties! Tell your family and/or executor where they can find the original copy of your will and any addendum(s). It's also a good idea to explain how your estate is to be distributed.

I know that estate planning inevitably entails contemplating your own demise, and that's not fun to think about, however, it's *really* important. You would undoubtedly want to have a say in what happens to your belongings, assets, and body in the event that you are no longer here.

I HAVE A WILL! WHAT NOW?

In addition to a will, you'll want to obtain a living will (also called an "advance healthcare directive") as well as a power of attorney agreement (POA). A living will is a written set of instructions for how you want to be medically treated and cared for if you are no longer able to make decisions due to incapacitation. It is meant to direct your doctors in a situation where the doctors cannot cure you and you cannot tell them what you want. It could be a situation where you have very little time to live and are being kept on life support. A living will can also appoint a friend or loved one as a legal decision maker on your behalf.

There are two types of power of attorney agreements: financial POA and healthcare POA.

A financial power of attorney is assigned to someone when you are ill or incapacitated. This can be for a short period of time or long-term. Having a financial power of attorney will enable someone to access your money to pay your bills, make investment decisions, and handle other financial matters for you. Conversely, a healthcare power of attorney agreement names someone who is legally able to make healthcare decisions for you.

Estate planning can spare your family from having to make difficult decisions on your behalf in the midst of a devastating situation. It's a very good idea to do both yourself and your loved ones a favor by making these decisions while you are healthy and able to think clearly to ensure your wishes are carried out if the need arises.

Although there are do-it-yourself websites, you may consider hiring an estate planning attorney to create these documents for you. If your estate is substantial and the arrangements are complicated, you definitely need an expert to navigate the tax implications and legal issues involved with estate planning.

CHAPTER SEVEN
COMPOUNDING INTEREST

GROW, GROW, GROW YOUR BOAT

If given the choice, would you rather have $1,000,000 or a penny doubled every day for a month? Most people I ask would choose the one million dollars. Chances are, you spent a second or two doing the math, and quickly figured that after a week, you would still only have $0.64. There's no need to keep calculating what the next three weeks would bring, right? The choice seems obvious!

Actually, it's a trick question. Assuming you, like most people, would prefer the larger sum of money, you'd be better off choosing the penny doubled. At the end of 30 days, you would have a whopping $5,368,709.12. It probably sounds hard to believe but this is a great example of the power of doubling, which is closely aligned in principle with the power of compounding.

Now that you are well on your way to achieving goals for your future, it's time to learn how the power of compounding interest can make a huge difference over the course of many years.

WHAT IS COMPOUNDING AND HOW DOES IT WORK?

For the purposes of a simplistic example, let's say you deposited $10,000 into an account that earns exactly 8% interest each year. By the end of the first year, your investment would be worth $10,800. If you took the $800 of earnings and "reinvested" it (in other words, added it to the original $10,000), the account would be worth $11,664 by the end of the second year. This is because the account earned 8% on $10,800 during the second year. The alternative would be earning 8% interest on the original $10,000, which would make the total earned at the end of two years $11,600. The extra $64 earned on the $800 return from the first year represents compounding. Granted, $64 doesn't sound like much, but the numbers begin growing at an astounding rate many years down the line.

My son opened a Roth IRA at the age of sixteen. He made small contributions into his Roth IRA each time he was paid from his job. He started off contributing $25 a paycheck and soon was able to increase his contributions to $50 a paycheck. Now that he's older and has a full-time job, he contributes much more to his Roth IRA each month. It has been really fun showing him the potential value of his Roth IRA when he is 65 years old if he maintains his current savings habit. It's a great way for him to see the reward of saving his money.

Let me illustrate why starting early is so important. Look at this example of three different people trying to reach the same goal of accumulating $1 million by the age of 65.

Kara, age 25, would need to invest $405 each month (assuming a hypothetical rate of return of 7%).

Adam, age 35, would need to invest $855 each month (assuming the same hypothetical rate of return of 7%).

Chris, age 45, would need to invest $1,970 each month (assuming the same hypothetical rate of return of 7%). That's nearly five times the amount Kara needs to invest each month!

MONTHLY INVESTMENT REQUIRED TO GET TO $1 MILLION AT AGE 65

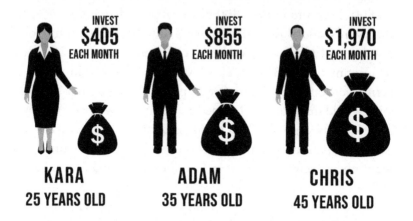

INVEST
$405
EACH MONTH

INVEST
$855
EACH MONTH

INVEST
$1,970
EACH MONTH

KARA
25 YEARS OLD

ADAM
35 YEARS OLD

CHRIS
45 YEARS OLD

Also consider that in order to achieve the same goal of having $1 million accumulated by age 65, Chris needs to save a total of $472,800 whereas Kara only has to save $194,400 because compound interest is doing the heavy lifting for her.

Now you can see how starting early is especially helpful when saving for retirement. Just setting aside a little money much earlier in your life can give you a tremendous head start and a powerful advantage.

HYPOTHETICAL SCENARIOS

Assume the following:

- You started to save $200 a month when you turned 16 years old and stopped when you turned 65 years old.
- Your annual rate of return averaged 8% from ages 16 to 65.

- You never took any withdrawals.

Can you guess what the account value would be at age 65? It would be $1.3 million! And to think you only deposited $117,600 over 49 years. It's amazing how the power of compounding can work in your favor!

Look at what happens if you wait to start saving. Let's say you chose not to start saving until age 30. In order to achieve the same account balance of $1.3 million you would have to save $610 a month from age 30 to age 65 with the same average rate of return of 8%.

Here is another example you might find relatable. Let's say your cell phone provider tells you that you're now eligible to buy a new cell phone. This time, instead of upgrading, you opt to keep your current phone. Instead of spending $1,000 on a new phone, you take that $1,000 and invest it for 30 years. Your rate of return averages 8% each year and you reinvest your dividends, just letting it grow without touching it. Guess how much you would have in 30 years? You would have $10,063! I encourage you to think about that the next time you are presented with the opportunity to purchase a new cell phone. Do you really need that cell phone or could you do something more productive with that money instead?

Another way to think about your money compounding is determining how many years it will take to double your money. The Rule of 72 is a useful formula that is famously used to estimate the number of years required to double the invested money at a given annual rate of return. The formula for the Rule of 72 is simple: just divide 72 by the rate of return.

Let's say your investments have an 8% annual rate of return. By using this formula, we can tell that it would take nine years to double your money (see the calculation on the next page).

RULE OF 72

Formula for Estimating How Long It Will Take for Your $ to Double

Just Divide 72 by the Rate of Return

$$\frac{72}{Rate\ of\ Return\ \%} = \begin{array}{c} Years \\ to \\ Double \end{array}$$

Example : 72 / 8 = 9 Years

Rate of Return	Number of Years to Double Your $
1%	72 Years
2%	36 Years
4%	18 Years
6%	12 Years
8%	9 Years
10%	7.2 Years
12%	6 Years
16%	4.5 Years
20%	3.6 Years

CHAPTER EIGHT

RETIREMENT

ENSURING LONG-TERM FINANCIAL FREEDOM

I've been a financial advisor for over a decade, and in that time I have met with countless people to discuss their retirement plans. I will never forget a woman named Paula who many years ago came to my office to tackle the financial logistics of her impending retirement. This was my first time meeting her, and when she initially sat down opposite me at my desk, her body language spoke volumes. With arms tightly crossed, shoulders hunched forward, and a severe expression on her face, she sat rigidly in the chair and appeared very much closed off. After ensuring the room temperature was to her satisfaction, I proceeded with the appointment as usual.

It came to light that she had concerns about the future. She didn't feel confident about her existing retirement plan, and she wasn't even sure she was going to be able to retire when she had planned, even though the selected date was on the horizon. She had no idea what her retirement would look like. I used sophisticated software to analyze her whole retirement plan with her, bit by bit, taking all of the variables into consideration. At last, the software projected that her chances of reaching her retirement goal were high, and that in the majority of scenarios, she would have plenty of money to cover her retirement spending. By the end of the appointment, a different woman was sitting across from me. She had sunk more comfortably into the chair, with her arms relaxed at her sides, and she had a huge smile of relief on her face.

Retirement is coming whether you plan for it or not. If you don't plan for it, you will be overwhelmed by it later.

WHEN SHOULD I START SAVING FOR RETIREMENT?

You should start as soon as you can. It is truly never too early. Ideally, you should start saving as soon as you start earning a paycheck, whether that's in high school with a part-time job or in your early twenties when you enter the workforce and begin earning a salary large enough to support yourself. The sooner you get started, the better. I cannot stress enough the impact of saving early, even if it doesn't seem like much money. Trust me, something is better than nothing and it all adds up.

Retirement may seem like a lifetime away to a young person. You might feel like it is something you don't need to plan for just yet. That's not true! Starting when you are young puts time on your side and builds good habits.

WHAT'S THE BEST WAY TO SAVE?

You can open your own individual retirement account (IRA), such as a traditional IRA or a Roth IRA.

Deposits (called contributions) put into a traditional IRA can be tax-advantaged in the year you make the deposit. If you contribute $6,000 to a traditional IRA this year, you may be able to deduct all or part of that amount from your income taxes for the year (provided you are under the income threshold). Then the money can grow for many years, but you will owe taxes when you withdraw the money from the account in retirement.

Unlike a traditional IRA, a $6,000 contribution made into a Roth IRA is taxed when you deposit the funds. You do not get a tax deduction for the year, however, the money compounds for years and when you finally withdraw it in retirement, you don't have to pay taxes on it.

In addition to IRAs, you may have access to a retirement savings account through your employer, often called a 401(k). Your employer may also offer a Health Savings Account (HSA). It's important to understand what these are, how they work, and how to take full advantage of them.

A 401(k) is an investment account. Contributions into your 401(k) are taken out of each paycheck before you even receive it. It's up to you to decide how much you want to contribute. Ask if your company has a 401(k) match or profit-sharing plan and if so, find out the details. With employer matching, your employer will contribute a certain amount of money in addition to what is taken out of your paycheck. You definitely don't want to miss out on an employer match. It's essentially free money! Even if you aren't in a position to contribute a lot to your 401(k), at least contribute as much as is required to take full advantage of the employer match. Profit sharing is when your employer chooses to distribute a portion of the company's profit into employees' 401(k) accounts. (Companies may choose to do this to lower their tax liability.)

Most 401(k) accounts function like a traditional IRA in that any contributions made to your 401(k) for the year get deducted from your taxable income. Sometimes employers also offer a Roth 401(k) option. Roth 401(k) accounts are far less prevalent than regular 401(k) accounts, but more and more employers these days are offering them as an alternative.

An HSA is a type of savings account that lets you set aside money on a pre-tax basis to pay for qualified medical expenses, which means you get to deduct any HSA contributions from your taxable income for the year. Like 401(k) contributions, HSA contributions made through an employer will be deducted from your paycheck before you receive it.

If you ask if it's too soon to start planning for retirement, the answer will always be a resounding *NO!* You will be much better off if you start saving as soon as you start earning an income. You definitely cannot create more time as needed down the road and you cannot borrow money for retirement like you would to buy a home. Get into the habit of saving money and making sound financial decisions *now*. It will make all the difference for your future retirement goal.

Let me show you an example so you can understand this. Say you put $6,000 into a retirement account each year until you're 65 and the account sees an 8% rate of return rounded to the nearest $1,000. (This is a hypothetical example and returns are not guaranteed.)

If you begin that savings pattern at age 45, you'll have $296,000 in your account when you turn 65.

If you begin saving at age 35, you'll end up with $734,000.

If you begin saving at age 25, you'll have $1,678,000 in your retirement account when you turn 65. Consider the amazing fact that if you started saving when you were 25, you will have contributed only $240,000 over the course of 40 years.

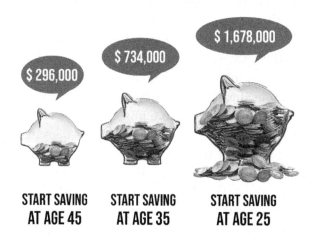

$ 296,000

$ 734,000

$ 1,678,000

START SAVING AT AGE 45   **START SAVING AT AGE 35**   **START SAVING AT AGE 25**

Which account balance would you prefer at age 65? If I had to venture a guess, I'd say the largest one! This is precisely why you should start early.

Considering what you've learned, what strategy would you choose to implement in your retirement savings goal? I encourage you to start as soon as possible. Don't wait!

A NOTE ABOUT GRATITUDE

When he was younger, I taught my son, Anthony, how important it is to give someone you meet a solid handshake, earnest eye contact, and respect. *Listen to what the person has to say, show genuine interest, and ask thoughtful questions,* I told him.

I also explained to him it is a lot easier learning from someone that has already experienced success and has wisdom to share than it is starting all over on your own and having to figure things out by yourself. I instilled in him the importance of properly thanking someone and expressing his gratitude for the time that individual spent helping him.

When Anthony was about six or seven years old, he had a pretty bad fall at a restaurant. He split open his forehead and ended up with several stitches. My friend, who was at the restaurant with us, accompanied us to the hospital.

Many years later, that same friend helped Anthony build a resume and gave him helpful tips on how to apply for a job at Boeing.

Upon his five-year anniversary of working at Boeing, Anthony put together a heartfelt thank you package complete with a gift card to the restaurant where he had taken that tumble years ago, and he mailed it to our longtime friend. I'm quite certain that this friend would do almost anything to help my son as a result of Anthony's thoughtful token of gratitude.

If you have an interest in a particular job or field of study, find people who have already traversed the road you're looking to go down; they will point out the potholes. Seek them out, ask them to lunch, show interest, learn from them, and most importantly, thank them! Whatever you do, don't convey your appreciation through a text message. A good, old-fashioned handwritten thank you card can go a long way.

Surround yourself with people who are positive and supportive. Avoid those who are negative and drag you down. Remember to be considerate to those who not only can help you, but who have also been there for you.

I feel certain that if you incorporate the lessons provided in this book, you'll be able to accomplish anything you set your mind to. My hope is that by reading this book, you've been inspired to take the steps necessary to build your best life!

ACKNOWLEDGMENTS

Thank you...

...to my incredibly supportive husband, Mark. From reading an early draft, to giving advice on the cover design, to making sure the house was quiet so I could focus, you played an important role in making sure this project got completed. Thank you so much, babe. I love you.

...to our youngest boys, Justin and Tyler, who willingly sat at the kitchen table and endured personalized, hands-on lessons about budgeting and goal-setting. Thank you to Justin for your editing suggestions and way to go Tyler for opening and funding a Roth IRA. I'm proud of you two!

...to our daughter, Brianna, whose keen insight, sense of humor, and readiness to lend an ear kept me sane throughout this process.

...to my tribe of friends who supported me along the way; most notably my dear friend Kris, who joined me at a three-day publishing workshop when this book was still a pipe dream, and my very close friend Donna, whose irrepressible enthusiasm for this project kept me going when I needed it most.

...to my Rotarian family for the support and sense of community they've given me, and especially to Randal Southam, owner of Southam Creative, who has provided invaluable guidance with regard to marketing strategies.

...to Debby Handrich of *coachdebby.com,* who encouraged me to share my personal story, successfully coaxing the strongest and most authentic version of my voice onto the page.

...to one of the most important people of this entire project, Michelle, who helped me more than anyone could imagine. Thank you for believing in me and taking a steadfast personal interest in this project from beginning to end. From multiple rounds of editing, to brainstorming how to spread my message, to listening to my frustrations and celebrating my victories, your passion for lending a hand is evident. I appreciate you more than words can express.

APPENDIX

Monthly Expenses	Monthly Budget Amount	Monthly Actual Amount	Difference
Housing			
Mortgage or Rent			
Homeowners or Renters Insurance			
Property Taxes			
Association Dues			
Home Repairs			
Landscaping/Housekeeping			
Total			
Utilities			
Electric/Gas/Oil			
Garbage			
Water/Sewer			
Cable/Satellite/Internet			
Phone/Cell Phone			
Netflix/Hulu			
Total			
Debt Repayment			
Vehicle Loan/Lease Payment			
Credit Card			
School Loan			
Other			
Total			
Person			
Toiletries			
Clothing			
Salon/Cosmetics			
Dry Cleanin'			
Subscriptions/M			
Pets-Food			
Char			
Gift			

Visit www.gofundyou.online for a free budget template.

DOWNLOAD THE FREE BUDGET TEMPLATE

Just to say thanks for buying my book, I would like to give you the Budget Template 100% FREE

TO DOWNLOAD GO TO:

https://gofundyou.online/budget

Made in the USA
Las Vegas, NV
28 December 2020